MINDFULNESS IN NATURE

BY AMBER BULLIS, MLIS

BLUE OWL
BOOKS

TIPS FOR CAREGIVERS

Social and emotional learning (SEL) helps children manage emotions, learn how to feel empathy, create and achieve goals, and make good decisions. One goal of teaching SEL skills can be to help children care for themselves, others, and the world around them. The more time children spend in nature, the more likely it is they will protect it in the future.

BEFORE READING

Talk to the reader about time spent outside.

Discuss: What are some activities you enjoy in nature? How does playing outside make you feel? Does your body feel different after playing outside? Do you experience different emotions?

AFTER READING

Talk to the reader about mindfulness and nature.

Discuss: What does it mean to be mindful in nature? Have you ever been mindful outside before? Did you learn any new ways to be mindful after reading this book?

SEL GOAL

Kids sometimes struggle with choosing to play outside. They may prefer spending time indoors, on digital devices. Try giving them examples of activities they can enjoy outdoors. Explain the importance of spending time outside every day. Consider moving appropriate lessons outside with an outdoor curriculum plan. Help your students experience nature in as many ways as possible.

TABLE OF CONTENTS

CHAPTER 1

WHAT IS MINDFULNESS?

Think about the last time you were outside. What did you see, hear, and smell? How did you feel? Being in nature is a perfect time to practice **mindfulness**!

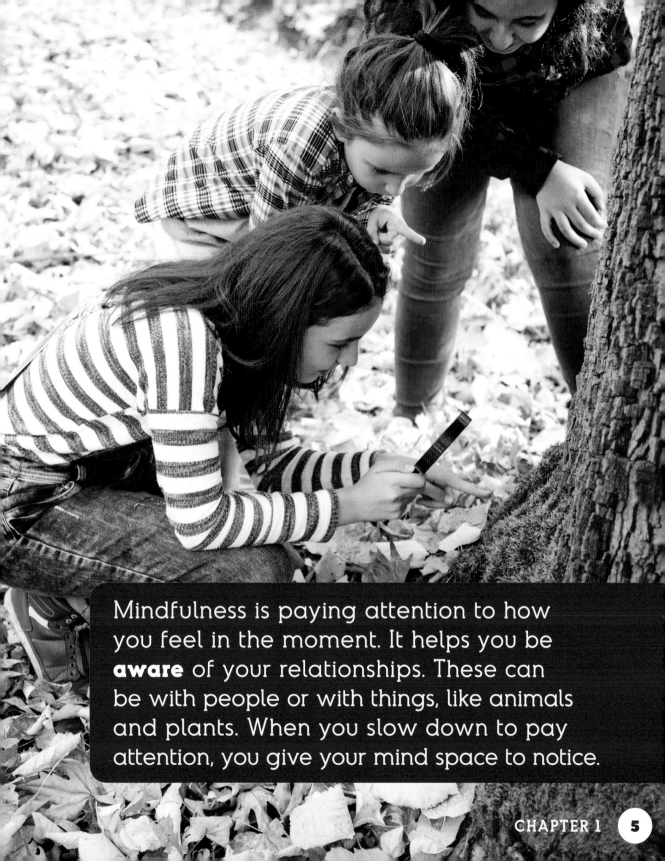

Mindfulness is paying attention to how you feel in the moment. It helps you be **aware** of your relationships. These can be with people or with things, like animals and plants. When you slow down to pay attention, you give your mind space to notice.

There is a lot to notice and **focus** on in nature. It appeals to our senses in a way **digital devices** can't. Put your devices away and take a walk. Look around you. Notice what you see. Notice what you smell. Do you feel wind or sunshine?

Then close your eyes and listen. What do you hear? Notice how your body and mind feel. This is practicing mindfulness!

CALMING NATURE

Being connected to nature can calm us. Scientific studies have found that we feel less **stress** in nature.

CHAPTER 2

HOW IT HELPS

Do you ever feel **overwhelmed**? It can be hard to let go of your worries.

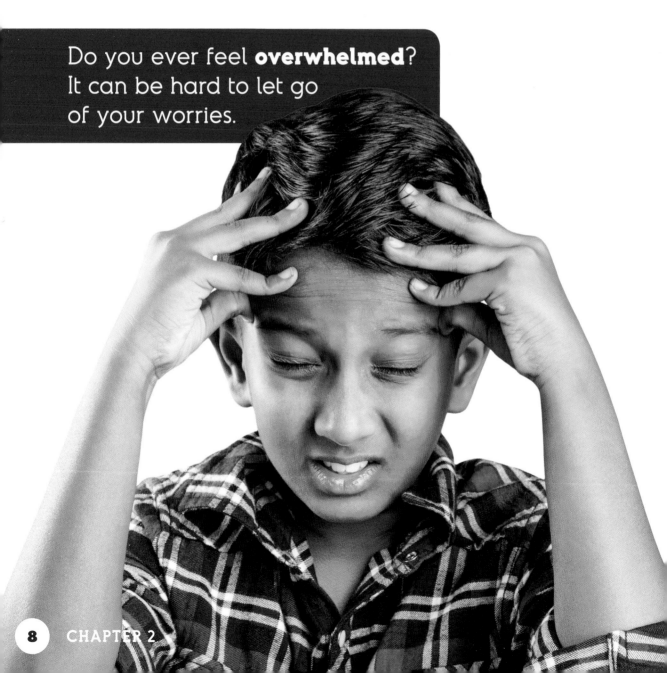

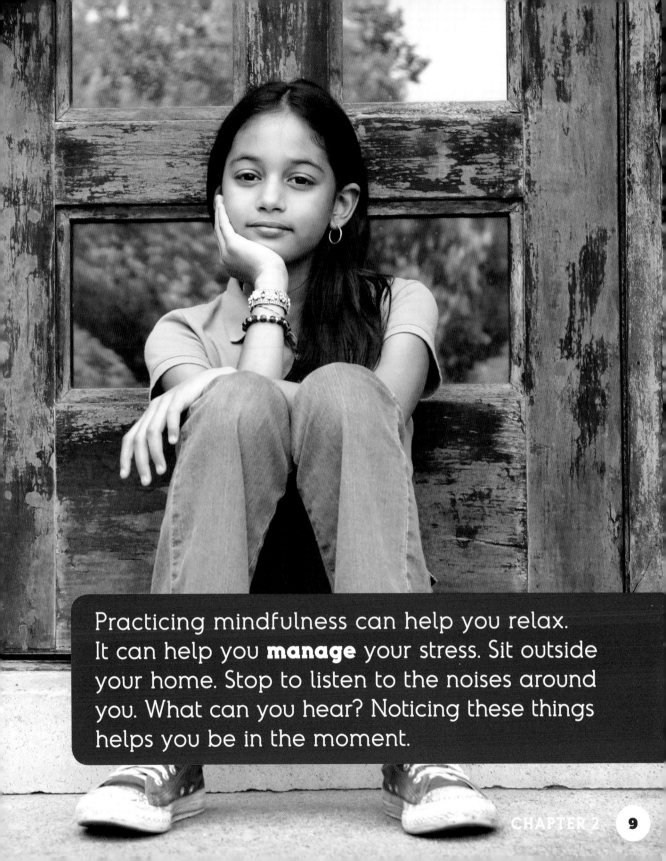

Practicing mindfulness can help you relax. It can help you **manage** your stress. Sit outside your home. Stop to listen to the noises around you. What can you hear? Noticing these things helps you be in the moment.

Did you have a hard day? Go outside and connect with nature. Swing on your favorite swing. Close your eyes, and take deep breaths of fresh air. Notice your surroundings.

It is OK if you find yourself thinking about your bad day. Redirect your mind to positive thoughts. How is being in nature helping you do this?

Notice your **environment**.
Look up. What do you see?
Are there shapes in the clouds?
Watch how they move.

How do you feel? Do you feel
calmer? Mindfulness is using
nature to connect with yourself.

Try growing a plant. Water it daily. Notice how the soil soaks up the water. Watch how it grows each day. Feel thankful and happy for what nature offers us.

WATCH IT GROW!

Do you have a garden? Or maybe there's a **community garden** or a **farmer's market** near you. Visit and notice how many things grow from Earth!

CHAPTER 3

PRACTICE IT!

Mindfulness in nature is being respectful of Earth and everything in it. Make posters about **recycling** to hang outside and at school.

Be a **steward** of the environment. This is putting mindfulness into action. Gather family and friends to clean the park. Pick up litter and throw it away or recycle it.

nature journal

sun was shining and warm

The wind made flowers sway in circles.

grass wet from dew

field in park

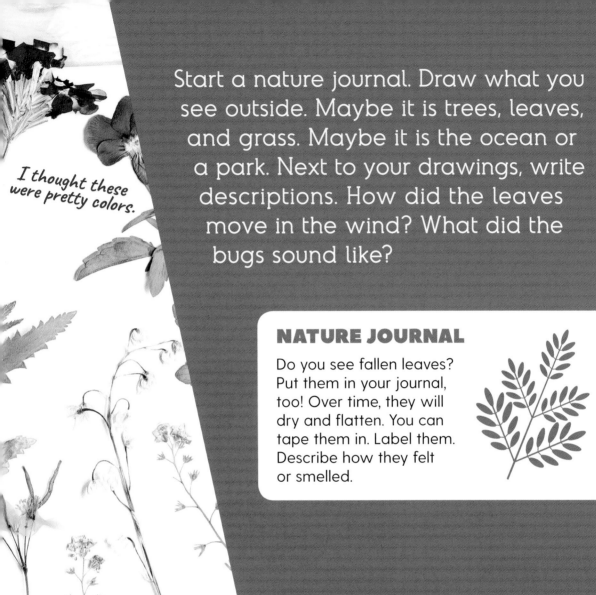

I thought these were pretty colors.

Start a nature journal. Draw what you see outside. Maybe it is trees, leaves, and grass. Maybe it is the ocean or a park. Next to your drawings, write descriptions. How did the leaves move in the wind? What did the bugs sound like?

NATURE JOURNAL

Do you see fallen leaves? Put them in your journal, too! Over time, they will dry and flatten. You can tape them in. Label them. Describe how they felt or smelled.

Find fun ways to be outside with your family and friends. You could go fishing or have a picnic with your family. You could play outdoor games with your friends.

Being outside feels good. It helps us be active and mindful. Be outside however you can! How will you be mindful in nature?

GOALS AND TOOLS

GROW WITH GOALS

There are many benefits to practicing mindfulness in nature.

Goal: Find some water! Being near water is a naturally relaxing experience during which you can practice mindfulness. The ocean, a lake, or even a fountain can help you feel more connected to nature.

Goal: Grow something! Taking care of a plant can help you be more mindful and respectful of the environment.

Goal: Read about nature! Find a book of poems about the outdoors. Your librarian can help.

MINDFULNESS EXERCISE

Go outside. Explore what's around you. Then sit and observe. Notice your thoughts and how you feel.

1. How does your body feel?

2. Do you feel any emotions? What are they?

3. Do any of your thoughts or feelings surprise you?

GLOSSARY

aware
Noticing and being conscious
of something.

community garden
A single piece of land that is
gardened by a group of people.

digital devices
Pieces of equipment with computers
inside, such as smartphones or tablets.

environment
The natural surroundings of living
things, such as the air, land, or sea.

farmer's market
A market at which local farmers
sell their agriculture products directly
to consumers.

focus
To concentrate on something.

manage
To work upon or try to alter.

mindfulness
A mentality achieved by focusing
on the present moment and calmly
recognizing and accepting your
feelings, thoughts, and sensations.

overwhelmed
Feeling completely overcome or
overpowered by thoughts or feelings.

recycling
Processing old items, such as glass,
plastic, or newspapers, so they can
be used to make new products.

steward
Someone who uses and protects
nature with conservation
and sustainable practices.

stress
Mental or emotional strain
or pressure.

TO LEARN MORE

FACT SURFER

Finding more information is as easy as 1, 2, 3.

1. Go to www.factsurfer.com

2. Enter "**mindfulnessinnature**" into the search box.

3. Choose your cover to see a list of websites.

INDEX

Blue Owl Books are published by Jump!, 5357 Penn Avenue South, Minneapolis, MN 55419, www.jumplibrary.com

Library of Congress Cataloging-in-Publication Data

Names: Bullis, Amber, author.
Title: Mindfulness in nature / by Amber Bullis.
Description: Blue Owl Books. | Minneapolis, MN: Jump!, Inc., [2020] | Series: Mindful me
Includes index. | Audience: Ages 7–10.
Identifiers: LCCN 2019022755 (print)
LCCN 2019022756 (ebook)
ISBN 9781645271758 (hardcover)
ISBN 9781645271765 (paperback)
ISBN 9781645271772 (ebook)
Subjects: LCSH: Nature–Psychological aspects–Juvenile literature.
Mindfulness (Psychology)–Juvenile literature.
Classification: LCC BF353.5.N37 B85 2020 (print)
LCC BF353.5.N37 (ebook) | DDC 155.4/1913–dc23
LC record available at https://lccn.loc.gov/2019022755
LC ebook record available at https://lccn.loc.gov/2019022756

Editor: Jenna Trnka
Designer: Molly Ballanger

Photo Credits: sianc/Shutterstock, cover; LightFieldStudios/iStock, 1; AlexussK/Shutterstock, 3; Roblan/Shutterstock, 4 (left); Diana_Badmaeva/Shutterstock, 4 (right); Daniela Jovanovska-Hristovska/iStock, 5; Zurijeta/Shutterstock, 6–7; StockImageFactory.com/Shutterstock, 8; DougSchneiderPhoto/iStock, 9; manonallard/iStock, 10–11; MediaProduction/iStock, 12–13; Anna Nahabed/Shutterstock, 14–15; denira/Shutterstock, 16 (left); Joanna Dorota/Shutterstock, 16 (middle); pearleye/iStock, 16 (right); Caiaimage/Trevor Adeiline/Getty, 17; Africa Studio/Shutterstock, 18–19; monkeybusinessimages/iStock, 20–21.

Printed in the United States of America at Corporate Graphics in North Mankato, Minnesota.